The Greatest Speeches of President John F. Kennedy

Titan Publishing

Edited by Brian R. Dudley

Titan Publishing books may also be purchased for educational, business, fundraising or promotional use. For information, please write to:

Titan Publishing
1225 East Sunset Drive #510, Bellingham WA 98226

Library of Congress Catalog Card Number: 95-90305

ISBN 1-887227-00-8

Printed at Vancouver, B.C.

Table of Contents

Introduction

A great deal has been written about John Fitzgerald Kennedy, both good and bad, since his death. But whether friend or foe, sympathetic or not, it is undeniable that JFK's emotional impact on Americans has been (and still is) greater than any President since. More than three decades have passed since that fateful day in Dallas, yet JFK's name stills pops up with astounding frequency. Why?

Perhaps JFK represents the loss of what could have been, or the nostalgia of simpler times. Or perhaps JFK's loss of life represents the country's loss of innocence. Whatever the reason, the spoken words of JFK suggest a heart-felt vision of America which may be lacking in contemporary politicians.

Despite being in office for fewer than three years, Kennedy led the country through many turbulent yet exhilarating times: the Bay of Pigs invasion, the Berlin Crisis, the Cuban Crisis, the Freedom Riders, the Civil Rights Bill, the decision to go to the moon, and the Nuclear Test Ban Treaty.

Kennedy's acceptance speech, delivered at the Los Angles Coliseum before 80,000 people and a television audience of 35 million, was JFK's first mention of the New Frontier. A phrase entirely of his making, JFK's 'New Frontier' came to be the clarion call of a generation. The 'New Frontier' speech was one of many stirring speeches delivered by JFK, some of which would come to be regarded as the most renowned in American history.

What follows on these pages is that history as defined by John Fitzgerald Kennedy.

Brian R. Dudley

July 15, 1960

Acceptance Speech at the 1960 Democratic Convention

Governor Stevenson, Senator Johnson, Mr. Butler, Senator Symington, Senator Humphrey, Speaker Rayburn, fellow Democrats: I want to express my thanks to Governor Stevenson for his generous and heart-warming introduction. It was my great honor to place his name in nomination at the 1956 Democratic Convention, and I am delighted to have his support and his counsel and his advice in the coming months ahead.

Let me say first that I accept the nomination of the Democratic Party. I accept it without reservation and with only one obligation - the obligation to devote every effort of my mind and spirit to lead our party back to victory and our nation to greatness. I am grateful too (applause) I am grateful too that you have provided us with such a strong platform to stand on and to run on.

Pledges which are made so eloquently are made to be kept. The "Rights of Man", the civil and economic rights essential to the human dignity of all men are indeed our goal and are indeed our first principle. This is a platform on which I can run with enthusiasm and with conviction. And I am grateful, finally, that I can rely in the coming months on many others. On a distinguished running mate, who brings unity and strength to our platform and our ticket, Lyndon Johnson. On one of the most articulate spokesmen of modern times, Adlai Stevenson. On a great fighter for our needs, as a nation and a people, Stuart Symington. On my travelling companion in Wisconsin and West Virginia, Senator Hubert Humphrey. On Paul Butler, our devoted and courageous chairman. And on that fighting campaigner whose support I now welcome, President Harry Truman. I feel a lot safer with all them on my side.

> "I hope that no American... will throw away his vote by voting either for me or against me because of my religious affiliation. It is not relevant"

And I am proud of the contrast with our Republican competitors. For their ranks are so thin that not one challenger has dared to put his head up in the last twelve months.

I am fully aware of the fact that the Democratic Party, by nominating someone of my faith, has taken on what many regard as a new and hazardous risk. New, at least, since 1928. The Democratic Party has once again placed its confidence in the American people, and in their ability to render a free and fair judgement, and in my ability to render a free and fair judgement. To uphold the constitution and my oath of office, to reject any kind of religious pressure or obligation that might directly or indirectly interfere with my conduct of the Presidency in the national interest. My record of 14 years in supporting public education, supporting complete separation of church and state, and resisting pressure from sources of any kind should be clear by now to anyone. I hope that no American, I hope that no American considering the really critical issues facing this country will waste his franchise and throw away his vote by voting either for me or against me because of my religious affiliation. It is not relevant.

I am telling you what you are entitled to know as I come before you seeking your support for the most powerful office in the free world. I am saying to you that my decisions on every public policy will be my own as an American, a Democrat and as a free man. I mention all of this only because this country faces so many serious challenges, so many great opportunities, so many burdens of responsibility, that I hope it is for those great matters that we can address ourselves in the coming months. And if this statement of mine makes it easier to concentrate on our nation's problems, then I am glad that I have made it.

Under any circumstances, the victory we seek in November will not be easy. We know that in our hearts. We know that our opponents will invoke the name of Abraham Lincoln on behalf of their candidate, despite the fact that his political career has often seemed to show charity towards none and malice for all. We know it will not be easy to campaign against a man who has spoken and voted on every side of every issue. Mr. Nixon may feel that it is his turn now after the New Deal and the Fair Deal. But before he deals, someone's going to cut the cards. That "someone" may be the millions of Americans who voted for President Eisenhower but would balk at electing his successor. For just as historians tell us that Richard I was not fit to fill the shoes of the bold Henry II and that Richard Cromwell was not fit to wear the mantle of his uncle (sic), they might add in future years that Richard Nixon did not measure up to the footsteps of Dwight D. Eisenhower.

Perhaps he can carry on the party policies, the policies of Nixon and Benson and Dirksen and Goldwater, but this nation cannot afford such a luxury. Perhaps we could afford a Coolidge following a Harding, and perhaps we could afford a Pierce following Fillmore, but after Buchanan this nation needed Lincoln, after Taft we needed Wilson and after Hoover we needed Franklin Roosevelt.

But we're not merely running against Mr. Nixon. Our task is not merely one of itemizing Republican failures. Nor is that wholly necessary. For the families forced from the farm do not need us to tell them of their plight. The unemployed miners and textiles workers know that the decision is before them in November. The old people without medical care, the families without a decent home, the parents of children without a decent school. They all know that it is time for a change.

We are not here to curse the darkness, we are here to light a candle. As Winston Churchill said on taking office some 20 years ago, if we open a quarrel between the present and the past, we shall be in danger of losing the future. Today our concern must be with that future. For the world is changing, the old era is ending, the old ways will not do. Abroad the balance of power is shifting, new and more terrible weapons are coming into use, one third of the world may be free, but one third is the victim of a cruel repression and the other third is rocked by poverty and hunger and disease. Communist influence has penetrated into Asia, it stands in the Middle East, and now festers some 90 miles off the coast of Florida. Friends have slipped into neutrality, and neutrals have slipped into hostilities. As our keynoter reminded us, the President who began his career by going to Korea ends it by staying away from Japan. The world has been close to war before, but now man, who survived all previous threats to his existence, has taken into his mortals hands the power to exterminate his species seven times over.

Here at home the future is equally revolutionary. The New Deal and the Fair Deal were bold measures for their generation. But now this is a new generation. A technological output and explosion on the farm has led to an output explosion. An urban population revolution has overcrowded our schools and cluttered our cities and crowded our slums. A peaceful revolution for human rights demanding an end to racial discrimination in all parts of our community life has strained at the leashes imposed by a timid executive leadership.

It is time in short, it is time in short for a new generation of leadership. All over the world particularly in the newer nations, young men are coming to power, men who are not bound by the traditions of the past, men who are not blinded by the old fears and hates and rivalries. Young men who can cast off the old slogans and the old delusions. The Republican nominee of course is a young man. But his approach is as old as McKinley. His party is the party of the past, the party of memory. His speeches are generalities from *Poor Richard's Almanac*. Their platform, their platform made up of old leftover Democratic planks, has the courage of our old convictions.

> "And we stand today on the edge of a new frontier - the frontier of the 1960's"

Their pledge is to the status quo. And today there is no status quo. For I stand here tonight facing west on what was once the last frontier. From the lands that stretched 3000 miles behind us, the pioneers gave up their safety, their comfort and sometimes their lives to build our new West. They were not the captives of their own doubts, nor the prisoners of their own price tags. They were determined to make the new world strong and free, an example to the world. To overcome its hazards and hardships. To conquer the enemies that threatened from within and without. Some would say that those struggles are all over. That all the horizons have been explored. That all the battles have been won. That there is no longer an American frontier. But I trust that no one in this assemblage would agree with that sentiment. For the problems are not all solved. And the battles are not all won. And we stand today on the edge of a new frontier - the frontier of the 1960's. The frontier of unknown opportunities and perils. The frontier of unfilled hopes and unfilled threats. Woodrow Wilson's New Freedom promised our nation a new political and economic framework. Franklin Roosevelt's New Deal promised security and succor to those in need.

But the new frontier of which I speak is not a set of promises - it is a set of challenges. It sums up not what I intend to offer of the American people, but what I intend to ask of them. It appeals to their pride, it appeals to our pride, not our security. It holds out the promise of more sacrifice instead of more security. The new frontier is here whether we seek it or not. Beyond that frontier are uncharted areas of science and space, unsolved problems of peace and war, unconquered problems of ignorance and prejudice, unanswered questions of poverty and surplus. It would be easier to shrink from that new frontier, to look to the safe mediocrity of the past, to be lulled by good intentions and high rhetoric, and those who prefer that course should not vote for me or the Democratic party.

But I believe that the times require imagination and courage and perseverance. I'm asking each of you to be pioneers towards that new frontier. My call is to the young at heart, regardless of age. To the stout in spirit, regardless of party, to all who respond to the scriptural call, "Be strong and of good courage; be not afraid, neither be dismayed". For courage not complacency is our need today. Leadership, not salesmanship. And the only valid test of leadership is the ability to lead and lead vigorously. "A tired nation" said David Lloyd George, "is a Tory nation". And the United States today can neither afford to be tired nor Tory.

There may be those who wish to hear more, more promises to this group or that, more harsh rhetoric about the men in the Kremlin as a substitute for policy, more assurances of a golden future where taxes are always low and the subsidies are always high, but my promises are in the platform that you have adopted. Our ends will not be won by rhetoric and we can have faith in the future only if we have faith in ourselves.

For the harsh facts of the matter are that we stand at this frontier at a turning point of history. We must prove all over again to a watching world, as we sit on a most conspicuous stage, whether this nation, conceived as it is, with its freedom of choice, its breadth of opportunity, its range of alternatives, can compete with the single-minded advance of the Communist system. Can a nation organized and governed such as ours endure? That is the real question. Have we the nerve and the will. Can we carry through in an age where we will witness not only new breakthroughs in weapons of destruction, but also a race for mastery of the sky and the rain, the ocean and the tides, the far side of space, and the inside of man's mind.

That is the question of the new frontier. That is the choice that our nation must make. A choice that lies not merely between two men, or two parties, but between the public interest and private comfort, between national greatness and national decline, between the fresh air of progress and the stale dank atmosphere of normalcy, between dedication or mediocrity. All mankind waits upon our decision. A whole world looks to see what we shall do, and we cannot fail that trust and we cannot fail to try.

It has been a long road from the first snowy day in New Hampshire many months ago, to this crowded convention city. Now begins another long journey taking me into your cities and homes across the United States. Give me your help and your hand and your voice. Recall with me the words of Isaiah that "They that wait upon the Lord shall renew their strength; they shall mount up with wings as eagles, they shall run and not be weary".

As we face the coming great challenge, we too shall wait upon the Lord and ask that He renew our strength. Then shall we be equal to the task. Then we shall not be weary. Then we shall prevail.

January 20, 1961

Inaugural Address at the White House

We observe today not a victory of party but a celebration of freedom - symbolizing an end as well as a beginning - signifying renewal as well as change. For I have sworn before you and Almighty God the same solemn oath our forebears prescribed nearly a century and three quarters ago.

The world is very different now. For man holds in his mortal hands the power to abolish all forms of human poverty and all forms of human life. And yet the same revolutionary beliefs for which our forebears fought are still at issue around the globe - the belief that the rights of man come not from the generosity of the state but from the hand of God.

We dare not forget today that we are the heirs of that first revolution. Let the word go forth from this time and place, to friend and foe alike, that the torch has been passed to a new generation of Americans - born in this century, tempered by war, disciplined by a hard and bitter peace, proud of our ancient heritage - and unwilling to witness or permit the slow undoing of those human rights to which this nation has always been committed, and to which we are committed today at home and around the world.

Let every nation know, whether it wishes us well or ill, that we shall pay any price, bear any burden, meet any hardship, support any friend, oppose any foe, to assure the survival and the success of liberty. This much we pledge - and more. To those old allies whose cultural and spiritual origins we share, we pledge the loyalty of faithful friends. United, there is little we cannot do in a host of cooperative ventures. Divided, there is little we can do - for we dare not meet a powerful challenge at odds and split asunder.

> "We shall pay any price, bear any burden, meet any hardship, support any friend, oppose any foe, to assure the survival and the success of liberty"

To those new states whom we welcome to the ranks of the free, we pledge our word that one form of colonial control shall not have passed away merely to be replaced by a far more iron tyranny. We shall not always expect to find them supporting our view. But we shall always hope to find them strongly supporting their own freedom - and to remember that in the past, those who foolishly sought power by riding the back of the tiger ended up inside.

To those peoples in the huts and villages of half the globe struggling to break the bonds of mass misery, we pledge our best efforts to help them help themselves, for whatever period is required - not because the Communists may be doing it, not because we seek their votes, but because it is right. If a free society cannot help the many who are poor, it cannot save the few who are rich.

To our sister republics south of our border, we offer a special pledge - to convert our good words into good deeds - in a new alliance for progress - to assist free men and free governments in casting off the chains of poverty. But this peaceful revolution of hope cannot become the prey of hostile powers. Let all our neighbors know that we shall join with them to oppose aggression or subversion anywhere in the Americas. And let every other power know that this hemisphere intends to remain the master of its own house.

To that world assembly of sovereign states, the United Nations, our last best hope in an age where the instruments of war have far outpaced the instruments of peace, we renew our pledge of support - to prevent it from becoming merely a forum for invective - to strengthen its shield of the new and the weak - and to enlarge the area in which its writ may run.

Finally, to those nations who would make themselves our adversary, we offer not a pledge but a request: that both sides begin anew the quest for peace, before the dark powers of destruction unleashed by science engulf all humanity in planned or accidental self-destruction.

We dare not tempt them with weakness. For only when our arms are sufficient beyond doubt can we be certain beyond doubt that they will never be employed.

But neither can two great and powerful groups of nations take comfort from our present course - both sides overburdened by the cost of modern weapons, both rightly alarmed by the steady spread of the deadly atom, yet both racing to alter that uncertain balance of terror that stays the hand of mankind's final war.

So let us begin anew - remembering on both sides that civility is not a sign of weakness, and sincerity is always subject to proof. Let us never negotiate out of fear. But let us never fear to negotiate.

Let both sides explore what problems unite us instead of belaboring these problems which divide us.

Let both sides, for the first time, formulate serious and precise proposals for the inspection and control of arms - and bring the absolute power to destroy other nations under the absolute control of all nations. Let both sides seek to invoke the wonders of science instead of its terrors. Together let us explore the stars, conquer the deserts, eradicate disease, tap the ocean depths, and encourage the arts and commerce.

Let both sides unite to heed in all corners of the earth the command of Isaiah - to "undo the heavy burdens [and] let the oppressed go free".

And if a beachhead of cooperation may push back the jungle of suspicion, let both sides join in creating a new endeavor, not a new balance of power, but a new world of law, where the strong are just and the weak secure and the peace preserved.

All this will not be finished in the first one hundred days. Nor will it finished in the first one thousand days, nor in the life of this administration, nor even perhaps in our lifetime on this planet. But let us begin.

In your hands, my fellow citizens, more than mine, will rest the final success or failure of our course. Since this country was founded, each generation of Americans has been summoned to give testimony to its national loyalty. The graves of young Americans who answered the call to service surround the globe.

Now the trumpet summons us again - not as a call to bear arms, though arms we need - not as a call to battle, though embattled we are - but as a call to bear the burden of a long twilight struggle, year in year out, "rejoicing in hope, patient in tribulation" - a struggle against the common enemies of man: tyranny, poverty, disease, and war itself.

Can we forge against these enemies a grand and global alliance, North and South, East and West, that can assure a more fruitful life for all mankind? Will you join in that historic effort?

In the long history of the world, only a few generations have been granted the role of defending freedom in its hour of maximum danger. I do not shrink from this responsibility - I welcome it. I do not believe that any of us would exchange places with any other people or any other generation. The energy, the faith, the devotion which we bring to this endeavor will light our country and all who serve it - and the glow from that fire can truly light the world.

> "And so, my fellow Americans: ask not what your country can do for you - ask what you can do for your country"

And so, my fellow Americans: ask not what your country can do for you - ask what you can do for your country.

My fellow citizens of the world: ask not what America will do for you, but what together we can do for the freedom of man.

Finally, whether you are citizens of America or citizens of the world, ask of us here the same high standards of strength and sacrifice which we ask of you. With a good conscience our only sure reward, with history the final judge of our deeds, let us go forth to lead the land we love, asking His blessing and His help, but knowing that here on earth God's work must truly be our own.

March 1, 1961

Statement by the President Upon Signing an Executive Order Establishing the Peace Corps

I have today signed an Executive Order providing for the establishment of a Peace Corps on a temporary pilot basis. I am also sending to Congress a message proposing authorization of a permanent Peace Corps. This Corps will be a pool of trained American men and women sent overseas by the U.S. Government or through private institutions and organizations to help foreign countries meet their urgent needs for skilled manpower.

It is our hope to have 500 or more people in the field by the end of the year.

The initial reactions to the Peace Corps proposal are convincing proof that we have, in this country, an immense reservoir of such men and women - anxious to sacrifice their energies and time to toil to the cause of world peace and human progress.

In establishing our Peace Corps we intend to make full use of the resources and talents of private institutions and groups. Universities, voluntary agencies, labor unions and industry will be asked to share in this effort - contributing diverse sources of energy and imagination - making it clear that the responsibility for peace is the responsibility of our entire society.

We will only send abroad Americans who are wanted by the host country - who have a real job to do - and who are qualified to do that job. Programs will be developed with care, and after full negotiation, in order to make sure that the Peace Corps is wanted and will contribute to the welfare of other people. Our Peace Corps is not designed as an instrument of diplomacy or propaganda or ideological conflict. It is designed to permit our people to exercise more fully their responsibilities in the great common cause of world development.

Life in the Peace Corps will not be easy. There will be no salary and allowances will be at a level sufficient only to maintain health and meet basic needs. Men and women will be expected to work and live alongside the nationals of the country in which they are stationed - doing the same work, eating the same food, talking the same language.

But if the life will not be easy, it will be rich and satisfying. For every young American who participates in the Peace Corps - who works in a foreign land - will know that he or she is sharing in the great common task of bringing to man that decent way of life which is the foundation of freedom and a condition of peace.

May 25, 1961

Special Message to the Congress on Urgent National Needs

Mr. Speaker, Mr. Vice President, my co-partners in Government, gentlemen and ladies:

The Constitution imposes upon me the obligation from "time to time give to the Congress information of the State of the Union". While this has traditionally been interpreted as an annual affair, this tradition has been broken in extraordinary times.

These are extraordinary times. And we face an extraordinary challenge. Our strength as well as our convictions have imposed upon this nation the role of leader in freedom's cause.

No role in history could be more difficult or more important. We stand for freedom. That is our conviction for ourselves - that is our only commitment to others. No friend, no neutral and no adversary should think otherwise. We are not against any man - or any nation - or any system - except as it is hostile to freedom. Nor am I here to present a new military doctrine, bearing any one name or aimed at any one area. I am here to promote the freedom doctrine.

(At this point the President spoke at length on foreign policy, civil defense, disarmament and lastly on space.)

Finally, if we are to win the battle that is now going on around the world between freedom and tyranny, the dramatic achievements in space which occurred in recent weeks should have made clear to us all, as did the Sputnik in 1957, the impact of this adventure on the minds of men everywhere, who are attempting to make a determination of which road they should take. Since early in my term, our efforts in space have been under review. With the advice of the Vice President, who is Chairman of the National Space Council, we have examined where we are strong and where we are not, where we may succeed and where we may not. Now it is time to take longer strides - time for a great new American enterprise - time for this nation to take a clearly leading role in space achievement, which in many ways may hold the key to our fortune on earth.

> "I believe this nation should commit itself to...landing a man on the moon"

I believe we possess all the resources and talents necessary. But the facts of the matter are that we have never made the national decisions or marshalled the national resources required for such leadership. We have never specified long-range goals on an urgent time schedule, or managed our resources and our time so as to insure their fulfillment.

Recognizing the head start obtained by the Soviets with their large rocket engines, which gives them many months of lead-time, and recognizing the likelihood that they will exploit this lead for some time to come in still more impressive successes, we nevertheless are required to make new efforts on our own. For while we cannot guarantee that we shall one day be the first, we can guarantee that any failure to make this effort will make us last. We take an additional risk by making it in full view of the world, but as shown by the feat of astronaut Shepard, this very risk enhances our stature when we are successful. But this is not merely a race. Space is open to us now; and our eagerness to share its meaning is not governed by the efforts of others. We go into space because whatever mankind must undertake, free men must fully share.

I therefore ask the Congress, above and beyond the increases I have earlier requested for space activities, to provide the funds which are needed to meet the following national goals:

First, I believe that this nation should commit itself to achieving the goal, before the decade is out, of landing a man on the moon and returning him safely to the earth. No single space project in this period will be more impressive to mankind, or more important for the long-range exploration of space; and none will be so difficult or expensive to accomplish. We propose to accelerate the development of the appropriate lunar space craft. We propose to develop alternate liquid and solid fuel boosters, much larger than any now being developed, until certain which is superior. We propose additional funds for other engine development and for unmanned explorations - explorations which are particularly important for one purpose which this nation will never overlook: the survival of the man who first makes this daring flight. But in a very real sense, it will not be one man who is going to the moon - if we make this judgement affirmatively, it will be an entire nation. For all of us must work to put him there.

Secondly, an additional 23 million dollars, together with 7 million dollars already available, will accelerate development of the Rover nuclear rocket. This gives promise of some day providing a means for even more exciting and ambitious exploration of space, perhaps beyond the moon, perhaps to the very end of the solar system itself.

Third, an additional 50 million dollars will make the most of our present leadership, by accelerating the use of space satellites for world-wide communications.

Fourth, an additional 75 million dollars - of which 53 million dollars is for the Weather Bureau - will help give us at the earliest possible time a satellite system for world-wide weather observation.

Let it be clear - and this is a judgement which the Members of the Congress must finally make - let it be clear that I am asking the Congress and the country to accept a firm commitment to a new course of action - a course which will last for many years and carry very heavy costs: 531 million dollars in fiscal '62 - an estimated seven to nine billion dollars additional over the next five years. If we are to go only half way, or reduce our sights in the face of difficulty, in my judgement it would be better not to go at all.

Now this is a choice which this country must make, and I am confident that under the leadership of the Space Committees of the Congress and the Appropriations Committees, that you will consider the matter carefully.

It is a most important decision that we make as a nation. But all of you have lived through the last four years and have seen the significance of space and the adventures in space, and no one can predict with certainty what the ultimate meaning will be of mastery of space.

I believe we should go to the moon. But I think every citizen of this country as well as the Members of the Congress should consider the matter carefully in making their judgement, to which we have given attention over many weeks and months, because it is a heavy burden, and there is no sense in agreeing or desiring that the United States take an affirmative position in outer space, unless we are prepared to do the work and bear the burdens to make it successful. If we are not, we should decide today and this year.

This decision demands a major national commitment of scientific and technical manpower, materiel and facilities, and the possibility of their diversion from other important activities where they are already thinly spread. It means a degree of dedication, organization and discipline which have not always characterized our research and developments efforts. It means we cannot afford undue work stoppages, inflated costs or material or talent, wasteful interagency rivalries, or a high turnover of key personnel.

New objectives and new money cannot solve these problems. They could in fact, aggravate them further - unless every scientist, every engineer, every serviceman, every technician, contractor, and civil servant gives his personal pledge that this nation will move forward, with the full speed of freedom, in the exciting adventure of space.

(President Kennedy concluded with remarks reiterating the body of his speech.)

July 25, 1961

Radio and Television Report to the Nation on the Berlin Crisis

Delivered from the President's Office at 10:00 pm

Good evening. Seven weeks ago tonight I returned from Europe to report on my meeting with President Khrushchev and the others. His grim warnings about the future of the world, his aide memoir on Berlin, his subsequent speeches and threats which he and his agents have launched, and the increase in the Soviet military budget that he has announced, have all prompted a series of decisions by the Administration and a series of consultations with the members of the NATO organization. In Berlin, as you recall, he intends to bring to an end, through a stroke of the pen, first our legal rights to be in West Berlin - and secondly our ability to make good on our commitment to the two million free people of that city. That we cannot permit.

> "The immediate threat to free men is in West Berlin"

We are clear about what must be done - and we intend to do it. I want to talk frankly with you tonight about the first steps that we shall take. These actions will require sacrifice on the part of many of our citizens. More will be required in the future. They will require, from all of us, courage and perseverance in the years to come. But if we and our allies act out of strength and unity of purpose - with calm determination and steady nerves - using restraint in our words as well as our weapons - I am hopeful that both peace and freedom will be sustained.

The immediate threat to free men is in West Berlin. But that isolated outpost is not an isolated problem. The threat is worldwide. Our effort must be equally wide and strong, and not be obsessed by any single manufactured crisis. We face a challenge in Berlin, but there is also a challenge in Southeast Asia, where the borders are less guarded, the enemy harder to find, and the dangers of communism less apparent to those who have so little. We face a challenge in our own hemisphere, and indeed wherever else the freedom of human beings is at stake.

Let me remind you that the fortunes of war and diplomacy left the free people of West Berlin, in 1945, 110 miles behind the Iron Curtain.

This map makes it very clear the problem that we face. The white is West Germany - the East is the area controlled by the Soviet Union, and as you can see from the chart, West Berlin is 100 miles within the area which the Soviets now dominate - which is immediately controlled by the so-called East German regime.

We are there as a result of our victory over Nazi Germany - and our basic rights to be there, deriving from that victory, include both our presence in West Berlin and the enjoyment of access across East Germany. These rights have been repeatedly confirmed and recognized in special agreements with the Soviet Union. Berlin is not part of East Germany, but a separate territory under the control of the allied powers. Thus our rights there are clear and deep-rooted. But in addition to those rights is our commitment to sustain - and defend, if need be - the opportunity for more than two million people to determine their own future and choose their own way of life.

Thus our presence in West Berlin, and our access thereto, cannot be ended by any act of the Soviet government. The NATO shield was long ago extended to cover West Berlin - and we have given our word that an attack upon that city will be regarded as an attack upon us all.

For West Berlin - lying exposed 110 miles inside East Germany, surrounded by Soviet troops and close to Soviet supply lines, has many roles. It is more than a showcase of liberty, a symbol, an island of freedom in a Communist sea. It is even more than a link with the Free World, a beacon of hope behind the Iron Curtain, an escape hatch for refugees.

West Berlin is all of that. But above all it has now become - as never before - the great testing place of Western courage and will, a focal point where our solemn commitments stretching back over the years since 1945, and Soviet ambitions now meet in basic confrontation.

It would be a mistake for others to look upon Berlin, because of its location, as a tempting target. the United States is there; the United Kingdom and France are there; the pledge of NATO is there - and the people of Berlin are there. It is as secure, in that sense, as the rest of us - for we cannot separate its safety from our own.

I hear it said that West Berlin is militarily untenable. And so was Bastogne. And so, in fact, was Stalingrad. Any dangerous spot is tenable if men - brave men - will make it so.

> "We cannot and will not permit the Communists to drive us out of Berlin, either gradually or by force"

We do not want to fight - but we have fought before. And others in earlier times have made the same dangerous mistake of assuming that the West was too selfish and too soft and too divided to resist invasions of freedom in other lands. Those who threaten to unleash the forces of war on a dispute over West Berlin should recall the words of the ancient philosopher: "A man who causes fear cannot be free from fear".

We cannot and will not permit the Communists to drive us out of Berlin, either gradually or by force. For the fulfillment of our pledge to that city is essential to the morale and security of Western Germany, to the unity of Western Europe, and to the faith of the entire Free World. Soviet strategy has long been aimed, not merely at Berlin, but at dividing and neutralizing all of

Europe, forcing us back on our own shores. We must meet our oft-stated pledge to the free peoples of West Berlin - and maintain our rights and their safety, even in the face of force - in order to maintain the confidence of other free peoples in our word and our resolve. The strength of the alliance on which our security depends is dependent in turn on our willingness to meet our commitments to them.

So long as the Communists insist that they are preparing to end by themselves unilaterally our rights in West Berlin and our commitments to its people, we must be prepared to defend those rights and those commitments. We will at all times be ready to talk, if talk will help. But we must also be ready to resist with force, if force is used upon us. Either alone would fail. Together, they can serve the cause of freedom and peace.

The new preparations that we shall make to defend the peace are part of the long-term build-up in our strength which has been underway since January. They are based on our needs to meet a world-wide threat, on a basis which stretches far beyond the present Berlin crisis. Our primary purpose is neither propaganda nor provocation - but preparation.

A first need is to hasten progress toward the military goals which the North Atlantic allies have set for themselves. In Europe today nothing less will suffice. We will put even greater resources into fulfilling those goals, and we look to our allies to do the same.

The supplementary defense build-ups that I asked from the Congress in March and May have already started moving us toward these and our other defense goals. They included an increase in the size of the Marine Corps, improved readiness of our reserves, expansion of air and sea lift, and stepped-up procurement of needed weapons, ammunition, and other items. To insure a continuing invulnerable capacity to deter or destroy any aggressor, they provided for the strengthening of our missile power and for putting 50% of our B-52 and B-47 bombers on a ground alert which would send them on their way with 15 minutes' warning.

These measures must be speeded up, and still others must now be taken. We must have sea and air lift capable of moving our forces quickly and in large numbers to any part of the world.

But even more importantly, we need the capability of placing in any critical area at the appropriate time a force which, combined with those of our allies, is large enough to make clear our determination and our ability to defend our rights at all costs - and to meet all levels of aggressor pressure with whatever levels of force are required. We intend to have a wider choice than humiliation or all-out nuclear action.

While it is unwise at this time either to call up or send abroad excessive numbers of these troops before they are needed, let me make it clear that I intend to take, as time goes on, whatever steps are necessary to make certain that such forces can be deployed at the appropriate time without lessening our ability to meet our commitments elsewhere.

Thus, in the days and months ahead, I shall not hesitate to ask the Congress for additional measures, or exercise any of the executive powers that I possess to meet this threat to peace. Everything essential to the security of freedom must be done; and if that should require more men, or more taxes, or more controls, or other new powers, I shall not hesitate to ask them. The measures proposed today will be constantly studied, and altered as necessary. But while we will not let panic shape our policy, neither will we permit timidity to direct our program.

Accordingly, I am now taking the following steps:

(1) I am tomorrow requesting the Congress for the current fiscal year an additional $3,247,000,000 of appropriations for the Armed Forces.

(2) To fill out our present Army Divisions, and to make more men available for prompt deployment, I am requesting an increase in the Army's total authorized strength from 875,000 to approximately 1 million men.

(3) I am requesting an increase of 29,000 and 63,000 men respectively in the active duty strength of the Navy and the Air Force.

(4) To fulfill these manpower needs, I am ordering that our draft calls be doubled and tripled in the coming months; I am asking the Congress for authority to order to active duty certain ready reserve units and individual reservists, and to extend tours of duty; and, under that authority, I am planning to order to active duty a number of air transport squadrons and Air National Guard tactical squadrons, to give us the airlift capacity and protection that we need. Other reserve forces will be called up when needed.

(5) Many ships and planes once headed for retirement are to be retained or reactivated, increasing our airpower tactically and our sealift, airlift, and anti-submarine warfare capability. In addition, our strategic air power will be increased by delaying the deactivation of B-47 bombers.

(6) Finally, some $1.8 billion - about half of the total sum - is needed for the procurement of non-nuclear weapons, ammunition and equipment.

The details on all these requests will be presented to the Congress tomorrow. Subsequent steps will be taken to suit subsequent needs. Comparable efforts for the common defense are being discussed with our NATO allies. For their commitment and interest are as precise as our own.

And let me add that I am well aware of the fact that many American families will bear the burden of these requests. Studies or careers will be interrupted; husbands and sons will be called away; incomes in some cases will be reduced. But these are burdens which must be borne if freedom is to be defended - Americans have willingly borne them before - and they will not flinch from the task now.

We have another sober responsibility. To recognize the possibilities of nuclear war in the missile age, without our citizens knowing what they should do and where they should go if bombs begin to fall, would be a failure of responsibility. In May, I pledged a new start on Civil Defense. Last week, I assigned, on the recommendation of the Civil Defense Director, basic responsibility for this program to the Secretary of Defense, to make certain it is administered and coordinated with our continental defense efforts at the highest civilian level. Tomorrow, I am requesting of the Congress new funds for the following immediate objectives: to identify and mark space in existing structures - public and private - that could be used for fall-out shelters in case of attack; to stock those shelters with food, water, first-aid kits and other minimum essentials for survival; to increase their capacity; to improve our air-raid warning and fall-out detection systems, including a new household warning system which is now under development; and to take other measures that will be effective at an early date to save millions of lives if needed.

In the event of an attack, the lives of those families which are not hit in a nuclear blast and fire can still be saved - if they can be warned to take shelter and if that shelter is available. We owe that kind of insurance to our families - and to our country. In contrast to our friends in Europe, the need for this kind of protection is new to our shores. But the time to start is now. In the coming months, I hope to let every citizen know what steps he can take without delay to protect his family in case of attack. I know that you will want to do no less.

(President Kennedy continued with remarks about the economy and the deficit)

> "In the event of an attack, the lives of those families which are not hit in a nuclear blast and fire can still be saved"

But I must emphasize again that the choice is not merely between resistance and retreat, between atomic holocaust and surrender. Our peace-time military posture is traditionally defensive; but our diplomatic posture need not be. Our response to the Berlin crisis will not be merely military or negative. It will be more than merely standing firm. For we do not intend to leave it to others to choose and monopolize the forum and the framework of discussion. We do not intend to abandon our duty to mankind to seek a peaceful solution.

As signers of the UN Charter, we shall always be prepared to discuss international problems with any and all nations that are willing to talk - and listen - with reason. If they have proposals - not demands - we shall hear them. If they seek genuine understanding - not concessions of our rights - we shall meet with them. We have previously indicated our readiness to remove any actual irritants in West Berlin, but the freedom of that city is not negotiable. We cannot negotiate with those who say "What's mine is mine and what's yours is negotiable". But we are willing to consider any arrangement or treaty in Germany consistent with the maintenance of peace and freedom, and with the legitimate security interests of all nations.

> "We seek peace - but we shall not surrender"

We recognize the Soviet Union's historical concern about their security in Central and Eastern Europe, after a series of ravaging invasions, and we believe arrangements can be worked out which will help to meet those concerns, and make it possible for both security and freedom to exist in this troubled area.

For it is not the freedom of West Berlin which is "abnormal" in Germany today, but the situation in that entire divided country. If anyone doubts the legality of our rights in Berlin, we are ready to have it submitted to international adjudication. If anyone doubts the extent to which our presence is desired by the people of West Berlin, compared to East German feelings about their regime, we are ready to have that question submitted to a free vote in Berlin and, if possible, among all the German people. And let us hear at that time from the two and one-half million refugees who have fled the Communist regime in East Germany - voting for Western-type freedom with their feet.

The world is not deceived by the Communist attempt to label Berlin as a hot-bed of war. There is peace in Berlin today. The source of world trouble and tension is Moscow, not Berlin. And if war begins, it will have begun in Moscow and not Berlin.

For the choice of peace or war is largely theirs, not ours. It is the Soviets who have stirred up this crisis. It is they who are trying to force a change. It is they who have opposed free elections. It is they who have rejected an all-German peace treaty, and the rulings of international law. And as Americans know from our history on our own old frontier, gun battles are caused by outlaws, and not by officers of the peace.

In short, while we are ready to defend our interests, we shall also be ready to search for peace - in quiet exploratory talks - in formal or informal meetings. We do not want military considerations to dominate the thinking of either East or West. And Mr. Khrushchev may find that his invitation to other nations to join in a meaningless treaty may lead to their inviting him to join in the community of peaceful men, in abandoning the use of force, and in respecting the sanctity of agreements.

While all of these efforts go on, we must not be diverted from our total responsibilities, from other dangers, from other tasks. If new threats in Berlin or elsewhere should cause us to weaken our program of assistance to the developing nations who are also under heavy pressure from the same source, or to halt our efforts for realistic disarmaments, or to disrupt or slow down our economy, or to neglect the education of our children, then those threats will surely be the most successful and least costly manoeuvre in Communist history. For we can afford all these efforts, and more - but we cannot afford not to meet this challenge.

And the challenge is not to us alone. It is a challenge to every nation which asserts its sovereignty under a system of liberty. It is a challenge to all those who want a world of free choice. It is a special challenge to the Atlantic Community - the heartland of human freedom.

We in the West must move together in building military strength. We must consult one another more closely than ever before. We must together design our proposals for peace, and labor together as they are pressed at the conference table. And together we must share the burdens and the risks of this effort.

The Atlantic Community, as we know it, has been built in response to challenge: the challenge of European chaos in 1947, of the Berlin blockade in 1948, the challenge of Communist aggression in Korea in 1950. Now, standing strong and prosperous, after an unprecedented decade of progress, the Atlantic Community will not forget either its history or the principles which gave it meaning.

The solemn vow each of us gave to West Berlin in time of peace will not be broken in time of danger. If we do not meet our commitments to Berlin, where will we later stand? If we are not true to our word there, all that we have achieved in collective security, which relies on these words, will mean nothing. And if there is one path above all others to war, it is the path of weakness and disunity.

Today, the endangered frontier of freedom runs through divided Berlin. We want it to remain a frontier of peace. This is the hope of every citizen of the Atlantic Community; every citizen of Eastern Europe; and, I am confident, every citizen of the Soviet Union. For I cannot believe that the Russian people - who bravely suffered enormous losses in the Second World War - would now wish to see the peace upset once more in Germany. The Soviet government alone can convert Berlin's frontier of peace into a pretext for war.

The steps I have indicated tonight are aimed at avoiding that war. To sum it all up: we seek peace - but we shall not surrender. That is the central meaning of this crisis, and the meaning of your government's policy.

With your help, and the help of other free men, this crisis can be surmounted. Freedom can prevail - and peace can endure.

I would like to close with a personal word. When I ran for the Presidency of the United States, I knew that this country faced serious challenges, but I could not realize - nor could any man realize who does not bear the burdens of this office - how heavy and constant would be those burdens.

"In the thermonuclear age, any misjudgment on either side about the intentions of the other could rain more devastation in several hours than has been wrought in all the wars of human history"

Three times in my lifetime our country and Europe have been involved in major wars. In each case serious misjudgments were made on both sides of the intentions of others, which brought about great devastation.

Now, in the thermonuclear age, any misjudgment on either side about the intentions of the other could rain more devastation in several hours than has been wrought in all the wars of human history.

Therefore I, as President and Commander-in-Chief, and all of us as Americans, are moving through serious days. I shall bear this responsibility under our Constitution for the next three and one-half years, but I am sure that we all, regardless of our occupations, will do our very best for our country, and for our cause. For all of us want to see our children grow up in a country at peace, and in a world where freedom endures.

I know that sometimes we get impatient, we wish for some immediate action that would end our perils. But I must tell you that there is no quick and easy solution. The Communists control over a billion people, and they recognize that if we should falter, their success would be imminent.

We must look to long days ahead, which if we are courageous and persevering can bring us what we all desire.

In these days and weeks I ask for your help, and your advice. I ask for your suggestions, when you think we could do better.

All of us, I know, love our country, and we shall all do our best to serve it. In meeting my responsibilities in these coming months as President, I need your good will, and your support - and above all, your prayers.

Thank you, and good night.

September 12, 1962

Address at Rice University on the Nation's Space Efforts

President Pitzer, Mr. Vice President, Governor, Congressman Thomas, Senator Wiley, and Congressman Miller, Mr. Webb, Mr. Bell, scientists, distinguished guests, and ladies and gentlemen:

I appreciate your president having made me an honorary visiting professor, and I will assure you that my first lecture will be very brief.

I am delighted to be here and I'm particularly delighted to be here on this occasion.

We meet at a college noted for knowledge, in a city noted for progress, in a State noted for strength, and we stand in need of all three, for we meet in an hour of change and challenge, in a decade of hope and fear, in an age of both knowledge and ignorance. The greater our knowledge increases, the greater our ignorance unfolds.

Despite the striking fact that most of the scientists that the world has ever known are alive and working today, despite the fact that this Nation's own scientific manpower is doubling every 12 years in a rate of growth more than three times that of our population as a whole, despite that, the vast stretches of the unknown and the unanswered and the unfinished still far outstrip our collective comprehension.

No man can fully grasp how far and how fast we have come, but condense, if you will, the 50,000 years of man's recorded history in a time span of but half a century. Stated in these terms, we know very little about the first 40 years, except at the end of them advanced man had learned to use the skins of animals to cover them. Then about 10 years ago, under this standard, man emerged from his caves to construct other kinds of shelters. Only 5 years ago man learned to write and use a cart with wheels. Christianity began less than 2 years ago. The printing press came this year, and then less than 2 months ago, during this whole 50-year span of human history, the steam engine provided a new source of power.

Newton explored the meaning of gravity. Last month electric lights and telephones and automobiles and airplanes became available. Only last week did we develop penicillin and television and nuclear power, and now if America's new spacecraft succeeds in reaching Venus, we will have literally reached the stars before midnight tonight.

This is a breathtaking pace, and such a pace cannot help but create new ills as it dispels old, new ignorance, new problems, new dangers. Surely the opening vistas of space promise high costs and hardships, as well as high reward.

So it is not surprising that some would have us stay where we are a little longer to rest, to wait. But this city of Houston, this State of Texas, this country of the United States was not built by those who waited and rested and wished to look behind them. This country was conquered by those who moved forward - and so will space.

William Bradford, speaking in 1630 of the founding of the Plymouth Bay Colony, said that all great and honorable actions are accompanied with great difficulties, and both must be enterprised and overcome with answerable courage.

If this capsule history of our progress teaches us anything, it is that man, in his quest for knowledge and progress, is determined and cannot be deterred. The exploration of space will go ahead, whether we join in it or not, and it is one of the great adventures of all time, and no nation which expects to be the leader of other nations can expect to stay behind in this race for space.

> "This city of Houston, this State of Texas, this country of the United States was not built by those who waited and rested and wished to look behind them. This country was conquered by those who moved forward - and so will space"

Those who came before us made certain that this country rode the first waves of the industrial revolutions, the first waves of modern invention, and the first wave of nuclear power, and this generation does not intend to founder in the backwash of the coming age of space. We mean to be a part of it - we mean to lead it. For the eyes of the world now look into space, to the moon and to the planets beyond, and we have vowed that we shall not see it governed by a hostile flag of conquest, but by a banner of freedom and peace. We have vowed that we shall not see space filled with weapons of mass destruction, but with instruments of knowledge and understanding.

Yet the vows of this Nation can only be fulfilled if we in this Nation are first, and, therefore, we intend to be first. In short, our leadership in science and in industry, our hopes for peace and security, our obligations to ourselves as well as others, all require us to make this effort, to solve these mysteries, to solve them for the good of all men, and to become the world's leading space-faring nation.

We set sail on this new sea because there is new knowledge to be gained, and new rights to be won, and they must be won and used for the progress of all people. For space science, like nuclear science and all technology, has no conscience of its own. Whether it will become a force for good or ill depends on man, and only if the United States occupies a position of pre-eminence can we help decide whether this new ocean will be a sea of peace or a new terrifying theatre of war. I do not say that we should or will go unprotected against the hostile misuse of space any more than we go unprotected against the hostile use of land or sea, but I do say that space can be explored and mastered without feeding the fires of war, without repeating the mistakes that man has made in extending his writ around this globe of ours.

There is no strife, no prejudice, no national conflict in outer space as yet. Its hazards are hostile to us all. Its conquest deserves the best of all mankind, and its opportunity for peaceful cooperation may never come again. But why, some say, the moon? Why choose this as our goal? And they may well ask why climb the highest mountain. Why, 35 years ago, fly the Atlantic? Why does Rice play Texas?

We choose to go to the moon. We choose to go to the moon in this decade and do the other things, not because they are easy, but because they are hard, because that goal will serve to organize and measure the best of our energies and skills, because that challenge is one that we are willing to accept, one we are unwilling to postpone, and one which we intend to win, and the others too.

> "We choose to go to the moon. We choose to go to the moon in this decade and do the other things, not because they are easy, but because they are hard"

It is for these reasons that I regard the decision last year to shift our efforts in space from low to high gear as among the most important decisions that will be made during my incumbency in the Office of the Presidency.

In the last 24 hours we have seen facilities now being created for the greatest and most complex exploration in man's history. We have felt the ground shake and the air shattered by the testing of a Saturn C-1 booster rocket, many times as powerful as the Atlas which launched John Glenn, generating power equivalent to 10,000 automobiles with their accelerators on the floor. We have seen the site where five F-1 rockets engines, each one as powerful as all eight engines of the Saturn combined, will be clustered together to make the advanced Saturn missile, assembled in a new building to be built at Cape Canaveral as tall as a 48-story structure, as wide as a city block, and as long as two lengths of this field.

Within these last 19 months at least 45 satellites have circled the earth. Some 40 of them were "made in the United States of America" and they were far more sophisticated and supplied far more knowledge to the people of the world than those of the Soviet Union.

The Mariner spacecraft now on its way to Venus is the most intricate instrument in the history of space science. The accuracy of that shot is comparable to firing a missile from Cape Canaveral and dropping it in this stadium between the 40-yard lines. Transit satellites are helping our ships at sea to steer a safer course. Tiros satellites have given us unprecedented warnings of hurricanes and storms, and will do the same for forest fires and icebergs.

We have had our failures, but so have others, even it they do not admit them. And they may be less public.

To be sure, we are behind, and will be behind for some time in manned flight. But we do not intend to stay behind, and in this decade we shall make up and move ahead.

The growth of our science and education will be enriched by new knowledge of our universe and environment, by new techniques of learning and mapping and observation, by new tools and computers for industry, medicine, the home as well as the school. Technical institutions, such as Rice, will reap the harvest of these gains.

And finally, the space effort itself, while still in its infancy, has already created a great number of new companies, and tens of thousands of new jobs. Space and related industries are generating new demands in investment and skilled personnel, and this city and the State, and this region, will share greatly in this growth. What was once the furthest outpost on the old frontier of the West will be the furthest outpost on the new frontier of science and space. Houston, your city of Houston, with its Manned Spacecraft Center, will become the heart of a large scientific and engineering community. During the next 5 years the National Aeronautics and Space Administration expects to double the number of scientists and engineers in this area, to increase its outlays for salaries and expenses to $60 million a year; to invest some $200 million in plant and laboratory facilities; and to direct or contract for new space efforts over $1 billion from this Center to this City.

> "As we set sail we ask God's blessing on the most hazardous and dangerous and greatest adventure on which man has ever embarked"

To be sure, all this costs us all a good deal of money. This year's space budget is three times what it was in January 1961, and it is greater than the space budget of the previous 8 years combined. That budget now stands at $5,400 million a year - a staggering sum, though somewhat less than we pay for cigarettes and cigars every year. Space expenditures will soon rise some more, from 40 cents per person per week to more than 50 cents a week for every man, woman and child in the United States, for we have given this program a high national priority - even though I realize that this is in some measure an act of faith and vision, for we do not know what benefits await us. But if I were to say, my fellow citizens, that we shall send to the moon, 240,000 miles away from the control station in Houston, a giant rocket more than 300 feet tall, the length of this football field, made of new metal alloys, some of which have not yet been invented, capable of standing heat and stresses several times more than have ever been experienced, fitted together with a precision better than the finest watch, carrying all the equipment needed for propulsion, guidance, control, communications, food and survival, on an untried mission, to an unknown celestial body, and then return it safely to earth, re-entering the atmosphere at speeds of over 25,000 miles per hour, causing heat about half that of the temperature of the sun - almost as hot as it is here today - and do all this, and do it right, and do it first before this decade is out, then we must be bold.

I'm the one who is doing all the work, so we just want you to stay cool for a minute. [laughter] However, I think we're going to do it, and I think that we must pay what needs to be paid. I don't think we ought to waste any money, but I think we ought to do the job. And this will be done in the decade of the sixties. It may be done while some of you are still here at school at this college and university. It will be done during the terms of office of some of the people who sit here on this platform. But it will be done. And it will be done before the end of this decade.

I am delighted that this university is playing a part in putting a man on the moon as part of a great national effort of the United States of America.

Many years ago the great British explorer George Mallory, who was to die on Mount Everest, was asked why did he want to climb it. He said, "Because it is there".

Well, space is there, and we're going to climb it, and the moon and the planets are there, and new hopes for knowledge and peace are there. And, therefore, as we set sail we ask God's blessing on the most hazardous and dangerous and greatest adventure on which man has ever embarked.

Thank you.

October 22, 1962

Radio and Television Report to the American People on the Soviet Arms Build-up in Cuba

Delivered from the President's Office at 7:00 pm

Good evening, my fellow citizens:

This Government, as promised, has maintained the closest surveillance of the Soviet military build-up on the island of Cuba. Within the past week, unmistakable evidence has established the fact that a series of offensive missile sites is now in preparation on that imprisoned island. The purpose of these bases can be none other than to provide a nuclear strike capability against the Western Hemisphere.

Upon receiving the first preliminary hard information of this nature last Tuesday morning at 9 a.m., I directed that our surveillance be stepped up. And having now confirmed and completed our evaluation of the evidence and our decision on a course of action, this Government feels obliged to report this new crisis to you in fullest detail.

> "This Government... has maintained the closest surveillance of the Soviet military build-up on the island of Cuba...a series of offensive missile sites is now in preparation on that imprisoned island"

The characteristics of these new missile sites indicate two distinct types of installations. Several of them include medium range ballistic missiles, capable of carrying a nuclear warhead for a distance of more than 1,000 nautical miles. Each of these missiles, in short, is capable of striking Washington, D.C., the Panama Canal, Cape Canaveral, Mexico City, or any other city in the southeastern part of the United States, in Central America, or in the Caribbean area.

Additional sites not yet completed appear to be designed for intermediate range ballistic missiles - capable of traveling more than twice as far - and thus capable of striking most of the major cities in the Western Hemisphere, ranging as far north as Hudson Bay, Canada, and as far south as Lima, Peru. In addition, jet bombers, capable of carrying nuclear weapons, are now being uncrated and assembled in Cuba, while the necessary air bases are being prepared.

This urgent transformation of Cuba into an important strategic base - by the presence of these large, long-range, and clearly offensive weapons of sudden mass destruction - constitutes an explicit threat to the peace and security of all the Americas, in flagrant and deliberate defiance of the Rio Pact of 1947, the traditions of this Nation and hemisphere, the joint resolution of the 87th Congress, the Charter of the United Nations, and my own public warnings to the Soviets on September 4 and 13. This action also contradicts the repeated assurances of Soviet spokesmen, both publicly and privately delivered, that the arms build-up in Cuba would retain its original defensive character, and that the Soviet Union had no need or desire to station strategic missiles on the territory of any other nation.

The size of this undertaking makes clear that it has been planned for some months. Yet only last month, after I had made clear the distinction between any introduction of ground-to-ground missiles and the existence of defensive antiaircraft missiles, the Soviet Government publicly stated on September 11 that, and I quote, "the armaments and military equipment sent to Cuba are designed exclusively for defensive purposes," that, and I quote the Soviet Government, "there is no need for the Soviet Government to shift its weapons...for a retaliatory blow to any other country, for instance Cuba," and that, and I quote their government, "the Soviet Union has so powerful rockets to carry these nuclear warheads that there is no need to search for sites for them beyond the boundaries of the Soviet Union". That statement was false.

Only last Thursday, as evidence of this rapid offensive build-up was already in my hand, Soviet Foreign Minister Gromyko told me in my office that he was instructed to make it clear once again, as he said his government had already done, that Soviet assistance to Cuba, and I quote, "pursued solely the purpose of contributing to the defense capabilities of Cuba," that, and I quote him, "training by Soviet specialists of Cuban nationals in handling defensive armaments was by no means offensive, and if it were otherwise," Mr. Gromyko went on, "the Soviet Government would never become involved in rendering such assistance." That statement also was false.

Neither the United States of America nor the world community of nations can tolerate deliberate deception and offensive threats on the part of any nation, large or small. We no longer live in a world where only the actual firing of weapons represents a sufficient challenge to a nation's security to constitute maximum peril. Nuclear weapons are so destructive and ballistic missiles are so swift, that any substantially increased possibility of their use or any sudden change in their deployment may well be regarded as a definite threat to peace.

"American citizens have become adjusted to living daily on the bull's-eye of Soviet missiles located inside the U.S.S.R. or in submarines. In that sense, missiles in Cuba add to an already clear and present danger"

For many years, both the Soviet Union and the United States, recognizing this fact, have deployed strategic nuclear weapons with great care, never upsetting the precarious status quo which insured that these weapons would not be used in the absence of some vital challenge. Our own strategic missiles have never been transferred to the territory of any other nation under a cloak of secrecy and deception; and our history - unlike that of the Soviets since the end of World War II - demonstrates that we have no desire to dominate or conquer any other nation or impose our system upon its people. Nevertheless, American citizens have become adjusted to living daily on the bull's-eye of Soviet missiles located inside the U.S.S.R. or in submarines.

In that sense, missiles in Cuba add to an already clear and present danger - although it should be noted the nations of Latin America have never previously been subjected to a potential nuclear threat.

But this secret, swift, and extraordinary build-up of Communist missiles - in an area well known to have a special and historical relationship to the United States and the nations of the Western Hemisphere, in violation of Soviet assurances, and in defiance of American and hemispheric policy - this sudden, clandestine decision to station strategic weapons for the first time outside of Soviet soil - is a deliberately provocative and unjustified change in the status quo which cannot be accepted by this country, if our courage and our commitments are ever to be trusted again by either friend or foe.

The 1930's taught us a clear lesson: aggressive conduct, if allowed to go unchecked and unchallenged, ultimately leads to war. This nation is opposed to war. We are also true to our word. Our unswerving objective, therefore, must be to prevent the use of these missiles against this or any other country, and to secure their withdrawal or elimination from the Western Hemisphere.

Our policy has been one of patience and restraint, as befits a peaceful and powerful nation, which leads a worldwide alliance. We have been determined not to be diverted from our central concerns by mere irritants and fanatics. But now further action is required - and it is under way; and these actions may only be the beginning. We will not prematurely or unnecessarily risk the costs of worldwide nuclear war in which even the fruits of victory would be ashes in our mouth - but neither will we shrink from that risk at any time it must be faced.

Acting, therefore, in the defense of our own security and of the entire Western Hemisphere, and under the authority entrusted to me by the Constitution as endorsed by the resolution of the Congress, I have directed that the following initial steps be taken immediately:

First: To halt this offensive build-up, a strict quarantine on all offensive military equipment under shipment to Cuba is being initiated. All ships of any kind bound for Cuba from whatever nation or port will, if found to contain cargoes of offensive weapons, be turned back. This quarantine will be extended, if needed, to other types of cargo and carriers. We are not at this time, however, denying the necessities of life as the Soviets attempted to do in their Berlin blockade of 1948.

Second: I have directed the continued and increased close surveillance of Cuba and its military build-up. The foreign ministers of the OAS, in their communique of October 6, rejected secrecy on such matters in this hemisphere. Should these offensive military preparations continue, thus increasing the threat to the hemisphere, further action will be justified. I have directed the Armed Forces to prepare for any eventualities; and I trust that in the interest of both the Cuban people and the Soviet technicians at the sites, the hazards to all concerned of continuing this threat will be recognized.

> "I call upon Chairman Khrushchev to halt and eliminate this clandestine, reckless, and provocative threat to world peace"

Third: It shall be the policy of this Nation to regard any nuclear missile launched from Cuba against any nation in the Western Hemisphere as an attack by the Soviet Union on the United States, requiring a full retaliatory response upon the Soviet Union.

Fourth: As a necessary military precaution, I have reinforced our base at Guantanamo, evacuated today the dependents of our personnel there, and ordered additional military units to be on a standby alert basis.

Fifth: We are calling tonight for an immediate meeting of the Organ of Consultation under the Organization of American States, to consider this threat to hemispheric security and to invoke articles 6 and 8 of the Rio Treaty in support of all necessary action. The United Nations Charter allows for regional security arrangements - and the nations of this hemisphere decided long ago against the military presence of outside powers. Our other allies around the world have also been alerted.

Sixth: Under the Charter of the United Nations, we are asking tonight that an emergency meeting of the Security Council be convoked without delay to take action against this latest Soviet threat to world peace. Our resolution will call for the prompt dismantling and withdrawal of all offensive weapons in Cuba, under the supervision of U.N. observers, before the quarantine can be lifted.

Seventh and finally: I call upon Chairman Khrushchev to halt and eliminate this clandestine, reckless, and provocative threat to world peace and to stable relations between our two nations. I call upon him further to abandon this course of world domination, and to join in an historic effort to end the perilous arms race and to transform the history of man. He has an opportunity now to move the world back from the abyss of destruction - by returning to his government's own words that it had no need to station missiles outside its own territory, and withdrawing these weapons from Cuba - by refraining from any action which will widen or deepen the present crisis - and then by participating in a search for peaceful and permanent solutions.

This Nation is prepared to present its case against the Soviet threat to peace, and our own proposals for a peaceful world, at any time and in any forum - in the OAS, in the United Nations, or in any other meeting that could be useful - without limiting our freedom of action. We have in the past made strenuous efforts to limit the spread of nuclear weapons. We have proposed the elimination of all arms and military based in a fair and effective disarmament treaty. We are prepared to discuss new proposals for the removal of tensions on both sides - including the possibilities of a genuinely independent Cuba, free to determine its own destiny. We have no wish to war with the Soviet Union - for we are a peaceful people who desire to live in peace with all other peoples.

But it is difficult to settle or even discuss these problems in an atmosphere of intimidation. That is why this latest Soviet threat - or any other threat which is made either independently or in response to our actions this week - must and will be met with determination. Any hostile move anywhere in the world against the safety and freedom of peoples to whom we are committed - including in particular the brave people of West Berlin - will be met by whatever action is needed.

Finally, I want to say a few words to the captive people of Cuba, to whom this speech is being directly carried by special radio facilities. I speak to you as a friend, as one who knows of your deep attachment to your fatherland, as one who shares your aspirations for liberty and justice for all. And I have watched and the American people have watched with deep sorrow how your nationalist revolution was betrayed - and how your fatherland fell under foreign domination. Now your leaders are no longer Cuban leaders inspired by Cuban ideals. They are puppets and agents of an international conspiracy which has turned Cuba against your friends and neighbors in the Americas - and turned it into the first Latin American country to become a target for nuclear war - the first Latin American country to have these weapons on its soil.

> "Our goal is not the victory of might, but the vindication of right - not peace at the expense of freedom, but both peace *and* freedom, here in this hemisphere and, we hope, around the world. God willing, that goal will be achieved"

These new weapons are not in your interest. They contribute nothing to your peace and well-being. They can only undermine it. But this country has no wish to cause you to suffer or to impose any system upon you. We know that your lives and land are being used as pawns by those who deny your freedom.

Many times in the past, the Cuban people have risen to throw out tyrants who destroyed their liberty. And I have no doubt that most Cubans today look forward to the time when they will be truly free - free from foreign domination, free to choose their own leaders, free to select their own system, free to own their own land, free to speak and write and worship without fear or degradation. And then shall Cuba be welcomed back to the society of free nations and to the associations of this hemisphere.

My fellow citizens: let no one doubt that this is a difficult and dangerous effort on which we have set out. No one can foresee precisely what course it will take or what costs or casualties will be incurred. Many months of sacrifice and self-discipline lie ahead - months in which both our patience and our will will be tested - months in which many threats and denunciations will keep us aware of our dangers. But the greatest danger of all would be to do nothing.

The path we have chosen for the present is full of hazards, as all paths are - but it is the one most consistent with our character and courage as a nation and our commitments around the world. The cost of freedom is always high - but Americans have always paid it. And one path we shall never choose, and that is the path of surrender or submission.

Our goal is not the victory of might, but the vindication of right - not peace at the expense of freedom, but both peace *and* freedom, here in this hemisphere and, we hope, around the world. God willing, that goal will be achieved.

Thank you and good night.

June 11, 1963

Radio and Television Report to the American People on Civil Rights

Delivered from the President's Office at 8:00 pm

Good evening, my fellow citizens: This afternoon, following a series of threats and defiant statements, the presence of Alabama National Guardsmen was required on the University of Alabama to carry out the final and unequivocal order of the United States District Court of the Northern District of Alabama. This order called for the admission of two clearly qualified young Alabama residents who happen to have been born Negro.

That they were admitted peacefully on the campus is due in good measure to the conduct of the students of the University of Alabama, who met their responsibilities in a constructive way.

I hope that every American, regardless of where he lives, will stop and examine his conscience about this and other related incidents. This nation was founded by men of many nations and backgrounds. It was founded on the principle that all men are created equal, and that the rights of every man are diminished when the rights of one man are threatened.

Today we are committed to a worldwide struggle to promote and protect the rights of all who wish to be free. When Americans are sent to Vietnam or West Berlin, we do not ask for whites only. It ought to be possible, therefore, for American students of any color to attend any public institution they select without having to be backed up by troops.

"Every American ought to have the right to be treated as he would wish to be treated, as one would wish his children to be treated. But this is not the case"

It ought to be possible for American consumers of any color to receive equal service in places of public accommodation, such as hotels and restaurants and theatres and retail stores, without being forced to resort to demonstration in the street. It ought to be possible for American citizens of any color to register and to vote in a free election without interference or fear of reprisal.

It ought to be possible, in short, for every American to enjoy the privileges of being American without regard to his race or his color. In short, every American ought to have the right to be treated as he would wish to be treated, as one would wish his children to be treated. But this is not the case.

The Negro baby born in America today, regardless of the section of the nation in which he is born, has about one half as much chance of completing high school as a white baby born in the same place on the same day, one third as much chance of completing college, one third as much chance of becoming a professional man, twice as much chance of becoming unemployed, about one seventh as much chance of earning $10,000 a year or more, a life expectancy which is seven years shorter, and the prospects of earning only half as much.

> "We face, therefore, a moral crisis as a country and as a people.... It is time to act"

This is not a sectional issue. Difficulties over segregation and discrimination exist in every city, in every state of the Union, producing in many cities a rising tide of discontent that threatens the public safety. Nor is this a partisan issue. In a time of domestic crisis men of goodwill and generosity should be able to unite regardless of party or politics. This is not even a legal or legislative issue alone. It is better to settle these methods in the courts than on the streets, and new laws are needed at every level, but law alone cannot make men see right.

We are confronted primarily with a moral issue. It is as old as the scriptures and is as clear as the American Constitution.

The heart of the question is whether all Americans are to be afforded equal rights and equal opportunities, whether we are going to treat our fellow Americans as we want to be treated. If an American, because his skin is dark, cannot eat lunch in a restaurant open to the public, if he can not send his children to the best public school available, if he cannot vote for the public officials who represent him, if, in short, he cannot enjoy the full and free life which all of us want, then who among us would be content to have the color of his skin changed and stand in his place? Who among us would be content with the counsels of patience and delay?

One hundred years of delay have passed since President Lincoln freed the slaves, yet their heirs, their grandsons, are not fully free. They are not yet freed from the bonds of injustice. They are not yet freed from social and economic oppression. And this nation, for all its hopes and all its boasts, will not be fully free until all its citizens are free.

We preach freedom around the world, and we mean it, and we cherish our freedom here at home; but are we to say to the world, and, much more importantly, to each other, that this is a land of the free except for the Negroes; that we have no second-class citizens except Negroes; that we have no class or caste system, no ghettos, no master race, except with respect to Negroes?

Now the time has come for this nation to fulfill its promise. The events in Birmingham and elsewhere have so increased the cries for equality that no city or state or legislative body can prudently choose to ignore them.

The fires of frustration and discord are burning in every city, North and South, where legal remedies are not at hand. Redress is sought in the streets, in demonstrations, parades, and protests which create tensions and threaten violence and threaten lives.

We face, therefore, a moral crisis as a country and as a people. It cannot be met by repressive police action. It cannot be left to increased demonstrations in the streets. It cannot be quieted by token moves or talk. It is a time to act in the Congress, in your state and local legislative bodies and, above all, in all of our daily lives.

It is not enough to pin the blame on others, to say this is a problem of one section of the country or another, or deplore the facts that we face. A great change is at hand, and our task, our obligation, is to make that revolution, that change, peaceful and constructive for all.

Those who do nothing are inviting shame as well as violence. Those who act boldly are recognizing right as well as reality.

Next week I shall ask the Congress of the United States to act, to make a commitment it has not fully made in this century to the proposition that race has no place in American life or law. The Federal judiciary has upheld that proposition in the conduct of its affairs, including the employment of federal personnel, the use of federal facilities, and the sale of federally financed housing.

But there are other necessary measures which only the Congress can provide, and they must be provided at this session. The old code of equity law under which we live commands for every wrong a remedy, but in too many communities, in too many parts of the country, wrongs are inflicted on Negro citizens and there are no remedies at law. Unless the Congress acts, their only remedy is in the street.

I am, therefore, asking the Congress to enact legislation giving all Americans the right to be served in facilities which are open to the public - hotels, restaurants, theatres, retail stores, and similar establishments.

This seems to me to be an elementary right. Its denial is an arbitrary indignity that no American in 1963 should have to endure, but many do.

I have recently met with scores of business leaders urging them to take voluntary action to end this discrimination, and I have been encouraged by their response. In the last two weeks over seventy-five cities have seen progress made in desegregating these kinds of facilities. But many are unwilling to act alone, and for this reason, nationwide legislation is needed if we are to move this problem from the streets to the courts.

I am also asking Congress to authorize the federal government to participate more fully in lawsuits designed to end segregation in public education. We have succeeded in persuading many districts to desegregate voluntarily. Dozens have admitted Negroes without violence. Today, a Negro is attending a state-supported institution in every one of our fifty states, but the pace is very slow.

Too many Negro children entering segregated grade schools at the time of the Supreme Court's decision nine years ago will enter segregated high schools this fall, having suffered a loss which can never be restored. The lack of an adequate education denies the Negro a chance to get a decent job.

The orderly implementation of the Supreme Court decision, therefore, cannot be left solely to those who may not have the economic resources to carry the legal action or who may be subject to harassment.

Other features will also be requested, including greater protection for the right to vote. But legislation, I repeat, cannot solve this problem alone. It must be solved in the homes of every American in every community across our country.

In this respect, I want to pay tribute to those citizens, North and South, who have been working in their communities to make life better for all. They are acting not out of a sense of legal duty but out of a sense of human decency. Like our soldiers and sailors in all parts of the world, they are meeting freedom's challenge on the firing line, and I salute them for their honor and courage.

My fellow Americans, this is a problem which faces us all - in every city of the North as well as the South. Today there are Negroes, unemployed - two or three times as many compared to whites - inadequate in education, moving into the large cities, unable to find work, young people particularly out of work without hope, denied equal rights, denied the opportunity to eat at a restaurant or lunch counter or go to a movie theatre, denied the right to a decent education, denied almost today the right to attend a State university even though qualified. It seems to me that these are matters which concern us all, not merely Presidents or congressmen or governors, but every citizen of the United States.

This is one country. It has become one country because all of us and all the people who came here had an equal chance to develop their talents.

We cannot say to ten percent of the population that you can't have that right; that your children can't have the chance to develop whatever talents they have; that the only way that they are going to get their rights is to go into the streets and demonstrate. I think we owe them and we owe ourselves a better country than that.

Therefore, I am asking for your help in making it easier for us to move ahead and to provide the kind of equality of treatment which we would want ourselves; to give a chance for every child to be educated to the limit of his talents. As I have said before, not every child has an equal talent or an equal ability or an equal motivation, but they should have the equal right to develop their talent and their ability and their motivation, to make something of themselves.

We have a right to expect that the Negro community will be responsible; will uphold the law, but they have a right to expect that the law will be fair, that the Constitution will be color blind, as Justice Harlan said at the turn of the century.

This is what we are talking about and this is a matter which concerns this country and what it stands for, and in meeting it I ask the support of all our citizens. Thank you very much.

June 26, 1963

Remarks by President Kennedy at the Berlin Wall

I am proud to come to this city as the guest of your distinguished Mayor, who has symbolized throughout the world the fighting spirit of West Berlin. And I am proud to visit the Federal Republic with your distinguished Chancellor, who for so many years has committed Germany to democracy and freedom and progress, and to come here in the company of my fellow American, General Clay, who has been in this city during its great moments of crisis and will come again if ever needed.

Two thousand years ago the proudest boast was "*civis Romanus sum*". Today, in the world of freedom, the proudest boast is "*Ich bin ein Berliner*".

I appreciate my interpreter translating my German!

There are many people in the world who really don't understand, or say they don't, what is the great issue between the Free World and the Communist world. Let them come to Berlin. There are some who say that communism is the wave of the future. Let them come to Berlin. And there are some who say in Europe and elsewhere we can work with the Communists. Let them come to Berlin. And there are even a few who say that it is true that communism is an evil system, but it permits us to make economic progress. "*Lass' sie nach Berlin kommen*". Let them come to Berlin!

"Two thousand years ago the proudest boast was '*civis Romanus sum*'. Today, in the world of freedom, the proudest boast is '*Ich bin ein Berliner*'"

Freedom has many difficulties and democracy is not perfect, but we have never had to put a wall up to keep our people in, to prevent them from leaving us. I want to say, on behalf of my countrymen, who live many miles away on the other side of the Atlantic, who are far distant from you, that they take the greatest pride that they have been able to share with you, even from a distance, the story of the last eighteen years. I know of no town, no city, that has been besieged for eighteen years that still lives with the vitality and the force and the hope and the determination of the city of West Berlin.

While the wall is the most obvious and vivid demonstration of the failures of the Communist system, for all the world to see, we take no satisfaction in it. For it is, as your Mayor has said, an offense not only against history but an offense against humanity, separating families, dividing husbands and wives and brothers and sisters, and dividing a people who wish to be joined together.

What is true of this city is true of Germany - real, lasting peace in Europe can never be assured as long as one German out of four is denied the elementary right of free men, and that is to make a free choice. In eighteen years of peace and good faith, this generation of Germans has earned the right to be free, including the right to unite their families and their nation in lasting peace, with goodwill to all people. You live in a defended island of freedom, but your life is part of the main. So let me ask you, as I close, to lift your eyes beyond the dangers of today to the hopes of tomorrow, beyond the freedom merely of this city of Berlin, or your country of Germany, to the advance of freedom everywhere, beyond the wall to the day of peace with justice, beyond yourselves and ourselves to all mankind.

Freedom is indivisible, and when one man is enslaved, all are not free. When all are free, then we can look forward to that day when this city will be joined as one, and this country, and this great Continent of Europe, in a peaceful and hopeful globe. When that day finally comes, as it will, the people of West Berlin can take sober satisfaction in the fact that they were in the front lines for almost two decades.

All free men, wherever they may live, are citizens of Berlin, and, therefore, as a free man, I take pride in the words "*Ich bin ein Berliner*".

July 26, 1963

Radio and Television Address to the Nation on the Nuclear Test Ban Treaty

Delivered from the President's Office at 7:00 pm

Good evening, my fellow citizens:

I speak to you tonight in a spirit of hope. Eighteen years ago the advent of nuclear weapons changed the course of the world as well as the war. Since that time, all mankind has been struggling to escape from the darkening prospect of mass destruction on earth. In an age when both sides have come to possess enough nuclear power to destroy the human race several times over, the world of communism and the world of free choice have been caught up in a vicious circle of conflicting ideology and interest. Each increase of tension has produced an increase of arms; each increase of arms has produced an increase of tension.

In these years, the United States and the Soviet Union have frequently communicated suspicion and warnings to each other, but very rarely hope. Our representatives have met at the summit and at the brink; they have met in Washington and in Moscow; in Geneva and at the United Nations. But too often these meetings have produced only darkness, discord, or disillusion.

> "For the first time, an agreement has been reached on bringing the forces of nuclear destruction under international control"

Yesterday a shaft of light cut into the darkness. Negotiations were concluded in Moscow on a treaty to ban all nuclear tests in the atmosphere, in outer space, and under water. For the first time, an agreement has been reached on bringing the forces of nuclear destruction under international control - a goal first sought in 1946 when Bernard Baruch presented a comprehensive control plan to the United Nations.

That plan, and many subsequent disarmament plans, large and small, have all been blocked by those opposed to international inspection. A ban on nuclear tests, however, requires on-the-spot inspection only for underground tests. This Nation now possesses a variety of techniques to detect the nuclear tests of other nations which are conducted in the air or under water, for such tests produce unmistakable signs which our modern instruments can pick up.

The treaty initialed yesterday, therefore, is a limited treaty which permits continued underground testing and prohibits only those tests that we ourselves can police. It requires no control posts, no onsite inspection, no international body.

We should also understand that it has other limits as well. Any nation which signs the treaty will have an opportunity to withdraw if it finds that extraordinary events related to the subject matter of the treaty have jeopardized its supreme interests; and no nation's right of self-defense will in any way be impaired. Nor does this treaty mean an end to the threat of nuclear war. It will not reduce nuclear stockpiles; it will not halt the production of nuclear weapons; it will not restrict their use in time of war.

Nevertheless, this limited treaty will radically reduce the nuclear testing which would otherwise be conducted on both sides; it will prohibit the United States, the United Kingdom, the Soviet Union, and all others which sign it, from engaging in the atmospheric tests which have so alarmed mankind; and it offers to all the world a welcome sign of hope.

For this is not a unilateral moratorium, but a specific and solemn legal obligation. While it will not prevent this Nation from testing underground, or from being ready to conduct atmospheric tests if the acts of others so require, it gives us a concrete opportunity to extend its coverage to other nations and later to other forms of nuclear tests.

This treaty is in part the product of Western patience and vigilance. We have made clear - most recently in Berlin and Cuba - our deep resolve to protect our security and our freedom against any form of aggression. We have also made clear our steadfast determination to limit the arms race. In three administrations, our soldiers and diplomats have worked together to this end, always supported by Great Britain. Prime Minister Macmillan joined with President Eisenhower in proposing a limited test ban in 1959, and again with me in 1961 and 1962.

But the achievement of this goal is not a victory for one side - it is a victory for mankind. It reflects no concessions either to or by the Soviet Union. It reflects simply our common recognition of the dangers in further testing.

This treaty is not the millennium. It will not resolve all conflicts, or cause the Communists to forego their ambitions, or eliminate the dangers of war. It will not reduce our need for arms or allies or programs of assistance to others. But it is an important first step - a step towards peace - a step towards reason - a step away from war.

Here is what this step can mean to you and to your children and your neighbors: First this treaty can be a step towards reduced world tension and broader areas of agreement. The Moscow talks have reached no agreement on any other subject, nor is this treaty conditioned on any other matter. Under-Secretary Harriman made it clear that any nonaggression arrangements across the division in Europe would require full consultation with our allies and full attention to their interests. He also made clear our strong preference for a more comprehensive treaty banning all tests everywhere, and our ultimate hope for general and complete disarmament. The Soviet Government, however, is still unwilling to accept the inspection such goals require.

No one can predict with certainty, therefore, what further agreements, if any, can be built on the foundations of this one. They could include controls on preparations for surprise attack, or on numbers and type of armaments. There could be further limitations on the spread of nuclear weapons. The important point is that efforts to seek new agreements will go forward.

But the difficulty of predicting the next step is no reason to be reluctant about this step. Nuclear test ban negotiations have long been a symbol of East-West disagreement. If this treaty can also be a symbol - if it can symbolize the end of one era and the beginning of another - if both sides can by this treaty gain confidence and experience in peaceful collaboration - then this short and simple treaty may well become an historic mark in man's age-old pursuit of peace.

"Let us make the most of this opportunity, and every opportunity, to reduce tension, to slow down the perilous nuclear arms race, and to check the world's slide toward final annihilation"

Western policies have long been designed to persuade the Soviet Union to renounce aggression, direct or indirect, so that their people and all people may live and let live in peace. The unlimited testing of new weapons of war cannot lead towards that end - but this treaty, if it can be followed by further progress, can clearly move in that direction.

I do not say that a world without aggression or threats of war would be an easy world. It will bring new problems, new challenges from the Communists, new dangers of relaxing our vigilance or of mistaking their intent.

But those dangers pale in comparison to those of the spiralling arms race and a collision course towards war. Since the beginning of history, war has been mankind's constant companion. It has been the rule, not the exception. Even a nation as young and as peace-loving as our own has fought through eight wars. And three times in the last two years and a half I have been required to report to you as President that this Nation and the Soviet Union stood on the verge of direct military confrontation - in Laos, in Berlin, and in Cuba.

A war today or tomorrow, if it led to nuclear war, would not be like any war in history. A full-scale nuclear exchange, lasting less than 60 minutes, with the weapons now in existence, could wipe out more than 300 million Americans, Europeans, and Russians, as well as untold numbers elsewhere. And the survivors, as Chairman Khrushchev warned the Communist Chinese, "the survivors would envy the dead". For they would inherit a world so devastated by explosions and poison and fire that today we cannot even conceive of its horrors. So let us try to turn the world away from war. Let us make the most of this opportunity, and every opportunity, to reduce tension, to slow down the perilous nuclear arms race, and to check the world's slide toward final annihilation.

Second, this treaty can be a step towards freeing the world from the fears and dangers of radioactive fallout. Our own atmospheric tests last year were conducted under conditions which restricted such fallout to an absolute minimum. But over the years the number and the yield of weapons tested have rapidly increased and so have the radioactive hazards from such testing. Continued unrestricted testing by the nuclear powers, joined in time by other nations which may be less adept in limiting pollution, will increasingly contaminate the air that all of us must breathe.

Even then, the number of children and grandchildren with cancer in their bones, with leukemia in their blood, or with poison in their lungs might seem statistically small to some, in comparison with natural health hazards. But this is not a natural health hazard - and it is not a statistical issue. The loss of even one human life, or the malformation of even one baby - who may be born long after we are gone - should be of concern to us all. Our children and grandchildren are not merely statistics toward which we can be indifferent.

Nor does this affect the nuclear powers alone. These tests befoul the air of all men and all nations, the committed and the uncommitted alike, without their knowledge and without their consent. That is why the continuation of atmospheric testing causes so many countries to regard all nuclear powers as equally evil; and we can hope that its prevention will enable those countries to see the world more clearly, while enabling all the world to breath more easily.

Third, this treaty can be a step toward preventing the spread of nuclear weapons to nations not now possessing them. During the next several years, in addition to the four current nuclear powers, a small but significant number of nations will have the intellectual, physical, and financial resources to produce both nuclear weapons and the means of delivering them. In time, it is estimated, many other nations will have either this capacity or other ways of obtaining nuclear warheads, even as missiles can be commercially purchased today.

I ask you to stop and think for a moment what it would mean to have nuclear weapons in so many hands, in the hands of countries large and small, stable and unstable, responsible and irresponsible, scattered throughout the world. There would be no rest for anyone then, no stability, no real security, and no chance of effective disarmament. There would only be the increased chance of accidental war, and an increased necessity for the great powers to involve themselves in what otherwise would be local conflicts.

If only one thermonuclear bomb were to be dropped on any American, Russian, or any other city, whether it was launched by accident or design, by a madman or by an enemy, by a large nation or by a small, from any corner of the world, that one bomb could release more destructive power on the inhabitants of that one helpless city than all the bombs dropped in the Second World War.

Neither the United States nor the Soviet Union nor the United Kingdom nor France can look forward to that day with equanimity. We have a great obligation, all four nuclear powers have a great obligation, to use whatever time remains to prevent the spread of nuclear weapons, to persuade other countries not to test, transfer, acquire, possess, or produce such weapons.

This treaty can be the opening wedge in that campaign. It provides that none of the parties will assist other nations to test in the forbidden environments. It opens the door for further agreements on the control of nuclear weapons, and it is open for all nations to sign, for it is in the interest of all nations, and already we have heard from a number of countries who wish to join with us promptly.

Fourth and finally, this treaty can limit the nuclear arms race in ways which, on balance, will strengthen our Nation's security far more than the continuation of unrestricted testing. For in today's world, a nation's security does not always increase as its arms increase, when its adversary is doing the same, and unlimited competition in the testing and development of new types of destructive nuclear weapons will not make the world safer for either side. Under this limited treaty, on the other hand, the testing of other nations could never be sufficient to offset the ability of our strategic forces to deter or survive a nuclear attack and to penetrate and destroy an aggressor's homeland.

> "Let us, if we can, step back from the shadows of war and seek out the way of peace. And if that journey is a thousand miles, or even more, let history record that we, in this land, at this time, took the first step"

We have, and under this treaty we will continue to have, the nuclear strength that we need. It is true that the Soviets have tested nuclear weapons of a yield higher than that which we thought to be necessary, but the hundred megaton bomb of which they spoke 2 years ago does not and will not change the balance of strategic power. The United States has chosen, deliberately, to concentrate on more mobile and more efficient weapons, with lower but entirely sufficient yield, and our security is, therefore, not impaired by the treaty I am discussing.

It is also true, as Mr. Khrushchev would agree, that nations cannot afford in these matters to rely simply on the good faith of their adversaries. We have not, therefore, overlooked the risk of secret violations. There is at present a possibility that deep in outer space, that hundreds and thousands and millions of miles away from the earth illegal tests might go undetected. But we already have the capability to construct a system of observation that would make such tests almost impossible to conceal, and we can decide at any time whether such a system is needed in the light of the limited risk to us and the limited reward to others of violations attempted at that range. For any tests which might be conducted so far out in space, which cannot be conducted more easily and efficiently and legally underground, would necessarily be of such a magnitude that they would be extremely difficult to conceal. We can also employ new devices to check on the testing of smaller weapons in the lower atmosphere. Any violations, moreover, involves, along with the risk of detection, the end of the treaty and the worldwide consequences for the violator.

Secret violations are possible and secret preparations for a sudden withdrawal are possible, and thus our own vigilance and strength must be maintained, as we remain ready to withdraw and to resume all forms of testing, if we must. But it would be a mistake to assume that this treaty will be quickly broken. The gains of illegal testing are obviously slight compared to their cost, and the hazard of discovery, and the nations which have initialed and will sign this treaty prefer it, in my judgment, to unrestricted testing as a matter of their own self-interests, for these nations, too, and all nations, have a stake in limiting the arms race, in holding the spread of nuclear weapons, and in breathing air that is not radioactive. While it may be theoretically possible to demonstrate the risks inherent in any treaty, and such risks in this treaty are small, the far greater risks to our security are the risks of unrestricted testing, the risk of a nuclear arms race, the risk of new nuclear powers, nuclear pollution, and nuclear war.

This limited test ban, in our most careful judgment, is safer by far for the United States than an unlimited nuclear arms race. For all these reasons, I am hopeful that this Nation will promptly approve the limited test ban treaty. There will, of course, be debate in the country and in the Senate. The Constitution wisely requires the advice and consent of the Senate to all treaties, and that consultation has already begun. All this is as it should be. A document which may mark an historic and constructive opportunity for the world deserves an historic and constructive debate.

It is my hope that all of you will take part in that debate, for this treaty is for all of us. It is particularly for our children and our grandchildren, and they have no lobby here in Washington. This debate will involve military, scientific, and political experts, but it must be not left to them alone. The right and the responsibility are yours.

If we are to open new doorways to peace, if we are to seize this rare opportunity for progress, if we are to be as bold and farsighted in our control of weapons as we have been in their invention, then let us now show all the world on this side of the wall and the other that a strong America also stands for peace. There is no cause for complacency.

We have learned in times past that the spirit of one moment or place can be gone in the next. We have been disappointed more than once, and we have no illusions now that there are shortcuts on the road to peace. At many points around the globe the Communists are continuing their efforts to exploit weakness and poverty. Their concentrations of nuclear and conventional arms must still be deterred.

The familiar contest between choice and coercion, the familiar places of danger and conflict, are all still there, in Cuba, in Southeast Asia, in Berlin, and all around the globe, still requiring all the strength and the vigilance that we can muster. Nothing could more greatly damage our cause than if we and our allies were to believe that peace has already been achieved, and that our strength and unity were no longer required.

But now, for the first time in many years, the path of peace may be open. No one can be certain what the future will bring. No one can say whether the time has come for an easing of the struggle. But history and our own conscience will judge us harsher if we do not now make every effort to test our hopes by action, and this is the place to begin. According to the ancient Chinese proverb, "A journey of a thousand miles must begin with a single step".

My fellow Americans, let us take that first step. Let us, if we can, step back from the shadows of war and seek out the way of peace. And if that journey is a thousand miles, or even more, let history record that we, in this land, at this time, took the first step.

Thank you and good night.

November 22, 1963

Remarks From An Undelivered Speech to the Dallas Citizen's Council

I am honored to have this invitation to address the annual meeting of the Dallas Citizens Council - joined by the members of the Dallas Assembly - and pleased to have this opportunity to salute the Graduate Research Center of the Southwest.

...There will always be dissident voices heard in the land, expressing opposition without alternatives, finding fault but never favor, perceiving gloom on every side and seeking influence without responsibility. These voices are inevitable.

But today, other voices are heard in the land - voices preaching doctrines wholly unrelated to reality, wholly unsuited to the Sixties, doctrines which apparently assume that words will suffice without weapons, that vituperation is as good as victory and that peace is a sign of weakness. At a time when the national debt is steadily being reduced in terms of its burden on our economy, they see that debt as the greatest single threat to our security. At a time when we are steadily reducing the number of federal employees serving every thousand citizens, they fear those supposed hordes of civil servants far more than the actual hordes of opposing armies.

> "We have achieved an increase of nearly 600 per cent in our special forces - those forces that are prepared to work with our allies and friends against the guerrillas, saboteurs, insurgents and assassins who threaten freedom in a less direct but equally dangerous manner"

...I want to discuss with you today the status of our strength and our security because this question calls for most responsible qualities of leadership and the most enlightened products of scholarship. For this nation's strength and security are not easily or cheaply obtained, nor are they quickly and simply explained. There are many kinds of strength and no one kind will suffice. Overwhelming nuclear strength cannot stop a guerrilla war. Formal pacts of alliance cannot stop internal subversion. Displays of material wealth cannot stop the disillusionment of diplomats subjected to discrimination.

Above all, words alone are not enough. The United States is a peaceful nation. And where our strength and determination are clear, our words need merely to convey conviction, not belligerence. If we are strong, our strength will speak for itself. If we are weak, words will be of no help.

...Finally, moving beyond the traditional roles of our military forces, we have achieved an increase of nearly 600 per cent in our special forces - those forces that are prepared to work with our allies and friends against the guerrillas, saboteurs, insurgents and assassins who threaten freedom in a less direct but equally dangerous manner.

...I have spoken of strength largely in terms of the deterrence and resistance of aggression and attack. But, in today's world, freedom can be lost without a shot being fired, by ballots as well as bullets. The success of our leadership is dependent upon respect for our mission in the world as well as our missiles, on a clearer recognition of the virtues of freedom as well as the evils of tyranny.

...And that is why we have regained the initiative in the exploration of outer space - making an annual effort greater than the combined total of all space activities undertaken during the 50s, launching more than 130 vehicles into earth orbit, putting into actual operation valuable weather and communications satellites, and making it clear to all that the United States of America has no intention of finishing second in space.

...My friends and fellow citizens; I cite these facts and figures to make it clear that America today is stronger than ever before. Our adversaries have not abandoned their ambitions - our dangers have not diminished - our vigilance cannot be relaxed. But now we have the military, the scientific and the economic strength to do whatever must be done for the preservation and promotion of freedom. That strength will never be used in pursuit of aggressive ambitions - it will always be used in pursuit of peace. It will never be used to promote provocations - it will always be used to promote the peaceful settlement of disputes.

We in this country, in this generation, are - by destiny rather than choice - the watchmen on the walls of world freedom. We ask, therefore, that we may be worthy of our power and responsibility; that we may exercise our strength with wisdom and restrain; and that we may achieve in our time and for all time the ancient vision of "peace on earth, good will toward men". That must always be our goal - and the righteousness of our case must always underlie our strength. For as was written long ago, "Except the Lord keep the city, the watchman waketh but in vain".

Editor's Note

President Kennedy never gave this speech, to be delivered at a luncheon at the Dallas Trade Mart. The President travelled in a motorcade from the airstrip at Love Field along a 10-mile route through downtown Dallas on his way to the Trade Mart. At approximately 12:30 pm, while passing the Texas School Book Depository, he was struck by several shots fired by at least one assassin. President Kennedy was pronounced dead at 1:00 pm at the Parkland Hospital in Dallas.

December 6, 1963

Remarks by President Johnson on Awarding the Presidential Medal of Freedom to President Kennedy

John Kennedy is gone. Each of us will know that we are the lesser for his death. But each is somehow larger because he lived. A sadness has settled on the world which will never leave it while we who knew him are still here.

The America that produced him shall honor him as well. As a simple gesture, but one which I know he would not have counted small, it is my privilege at this moment to award the Presidential Medal of Freedom posthumously to John Fitzgerald Kennedy on behalf of the great Republic for which he lived and died.

The citation reads:

> John Fitzgerald Kennedy, 35th President of the United States, soldier, scholar, statesman, defender of freedom, pioneer for peace, author of hope - combining courage with reason, and combating hate with compassion, he led the land he loved toward new frontiers of opportunity for all men and peace for all time. Beloved in a life of selfless service, mourned by all in a death of senseless crime, the energy, faith and devotion which he brought to his extraordinarily successful though tragically brief endeavors will hereafter "light our country and all who serve it - and the glow from that fire can truly light the world".

Quick JFK Facts

John Fitzgerald Kennedy
35th President of the United States (1961-1963)

Nicknames:	"Jack"; "JFK".
Born:	May 29, 1917 in Brookline, Massachusetts.
Education:	Harvard College, graduated in 1940.
Profession:	Author, Public Servant.
Religion:	Roman Catholic.
Marriage:	September 12, 1953, to Jacqueline Bouvier (1929-94).
Children:	Caroline Bouvier Kennedy (1957-); John Fitzgerald Kennedy; (1960-); Patrick Bouvier Kennedy (1963).
Writings:	Why England Slept (1940); Profiles in Courage (1956).
Political Affiliation:	Democrat.
Died:	November 22, 1963 in Dallas, Texas.
Buried:	Arlington National Cemetery, Arlington, Virginia.
Vice-President:	Lyndon Baines Johnson.